CHAPTER

BY

CHAPTER

VOCABULARY AND COMPREHENSION

© 2023 Doris McKelvey

CONTENTS

Novel Titles	Reading Level

Tales of a Fourth Grade Nothing	3.3
The Whipping Boy	3.9
Donavan's Word Jar	4.1
Code 7: Cracking the Code for an Epic Life	4.3
Charlotte's Web	4.4
The Chocolate Touch	4.7
Sophie Washington: Queen of the Bee	5.0
The Mouse and the Motorcycle	5.1
Ralph S. Mouse	5.1
Hatchet	5.7
The Real Thief	6.1

ABOUT THE AUTHOR

Greetings!

I am a retired teacher and ELAR Instructional Coach with 33 years experience in education.

As an IC, I provided professional development for teachers K-5 on my campus during weekly PLC meetings, organized by grade level.

I trained teachers on how to use novels effectively for book clubs, literature circles, book discussions, independent reading, and guided reading groups.

Often, I would walk into a classroom and join a group of students already reading together. It was a good way to interact with students, provide assistance, and build relationships.

Also, teachers would schedule time for me to come into their classroom to model. We would meet later for feedback and collaboration.

Chapter by Chapter was created to promote student success in reading!

Use it as a tool for student accountability for independent reading, interventions, one-on-one tutoring, or in a manner that fits the needs of your classroom.

mckelvey.doris@yahoo.com

TALES OF A FOURTH GRADE NOTHING

By Judy Blume

Living with his little brother, Fudge, makes Peter Hatcher feel like a fourth grade nothing.

CHAPTER 1 THE BIG WINNER

1. What did Peter win at the birthday party?

    A. A basketball to dribble

    B. A turtle

    C. A goldfish

CHAPTER 2 MR. AND MRS. JUICY-O

There was no **point** in arguing. Mom wasn't going to change her mind.

2. What is the meaning of the word **point** in this sentence?

    A. The sharp or tapered end of something

    B. In printing or writing, a dot or decimal

    C. Purpose or advantage

    D. A narrow piece of land extending into water; cape

3. Why did Peter say, "Thank you, very much," for the picture dictionary?

    A. It was what he always wanted!

    B. He wanted to be polite.

    C. Fudge had destroyed his other book.

Mrs. Yarby said, "It's silly to keep it if you already have one." She sounded **insulted**. Like it was my fault she brought me something I already had.

4. What is the meaning of the word **insulted** in this sentence?
    A. Humiliated
    B. Praised
    C. happy

I **inspected** my turtle all over. He seemed all right.

5. What does the word **inspected** mean in this sentence?
    A. Dishonored
    B. Examined
    C. Petted

6. What did Fudge do to the Yarby's suitcase?
    A. Decorated it with one hundred green stamps
    B. Poured Juicy-o all over it
    C. Colored it with crayons

CHAPTER 3   THE FAMILY DOG

My father is in **charge** of the TV commercial for Toddle Bike company.

7. What is the meaning of **charge** in this sentence?

    A. To ask for as a price, cost, or purchase

    B. To accuse

    C. To attack or rush upon violently

    D. To entrust with a duty or task

    E. To fill with electricity as a battery

I learned to stand on my head in gym class. I showed my mother, my father, and Fudge. They were all **impressed** that I could stay up for three minutes.

8. Which word means the **same** as **impressed**?

    A. Troubled

    B. Fascinated

    C. Concerned

9. What did Peter's dad do to Fudge **because** he would not eat.

   A. He spanked Fudge.

   B. He cooked his favorite meal.

   C. He dumped a whole bowl of cereal over Fudge's head.

And for a long time after that Fudge's favorite **expression** was, "eat it or wear it!"

10. What does the word **expression** mean?

    A. Particular choice of word or phrase

    B. Silence

    C. Combination of variables for calculating value

CHAPTER 4   MY BROTHER THE BIRD

Me and Jimmy like to play secret agent in the park. Jimmy can **imitate** all kinds of foreign accents. Probably because his father is a part time actor.

11. What is the meaning of the word **imitate** in this sentence?

    A. Create different sounds

    B. To mimic or impersonate

    C. Teach a class at city College like his father

My mother **hesitated**. "I don't know," she said. "I've never left Fudge before."

12. What does the word **hesitate** mean in this sentence?

    A. Be reluctant, wait

    B. Be hasty

    C. Decide quickly

13. What happened **because** Fudge thought he was a bird?

    A. Mrs. Hatcher yelled at Sheila.

    B. Peter and Jimmy had an argument.

    C. He tried to fly from the jungle gym and fell.

CHAPTER 5 THE BIRTHDAY BASH

My mother **snapped** a picture of them in their party hats with a new camera.

14. What does the word **snapped** mean in this sentence?

    A. Uttered sharply and quickly as a command

    B. Photographed quickly

    C. Broken suddenly with a crackling sound

15. Why did Peter call his brother Fang?

   A. Because when Fudge smiles, all you can see are the top two side teeth next to the big space, so it looks like he has fangs

   B. Because Fudge likes to wear plastic teeth in his mouth

   C. Because Fudge collects stuffed animal of snakes as pets

My mother selected a picture book from Fudge's bookshelf. "I heard that one!" Jennie said when she saw the **cover**.

16. What does **cover** mean in this sentence?

   A. To place over for protection or to hide it

   B. In sports, to guard an opponent

   C. The binding of a book or magazine

CHAPTER 6   FANG HITS TOWN

He smeared mashed potatoes on the wall. "Fudgie! That's **naughty**," said mom.

17. Which word means the **same** as n**aughty**?

   A. Misbehaving

   B. Obedient

   C. Pleasant

   D. Dazzled

CHAPTER 7   THE FLYING TRAIN COMMITTEE

18. Why did the truck on the poster look like a flying train?

    A. Because Peter and Jimmy were not good artists

    B. Because the ground had not been drawn under it yet

    C. Because the ship was drawn too big on the poster

My mother put the poster on top of the refrigerator so it would be **safe** until the next day, when I would take it to school.

19. Which is the **correct** meaning of **safe** in this sentence?

    A. A strong metal box for protecting valuables

    B. Free from danger or evil

    C. In baseball, having reached the base without being out

CHAPTER 8   THE TV STAR

"You mean only one out of all these kids is going to be **picked**?

20. Which is the **correct** meaning for the word **picked** in this sentence?
    A. To pluck the strings of a guitar
    B. Choose or select
    C. To open a lock by other means than a key
    D. A pointed metal tool with a double head and a wooden handle used for breaking ground, rocks

21. What is the **problem** in this chapter?
    A. Janet ran out of Oreo cookies.
    B. Fudge would not ride the bike for the cameraman.
    C. Peter rode the Toddle-Bike.

22. How was the problem **solved**?
    A. Fudge was given one cookie.
    B. Father pulled Fudge off the bike.
    C. Fudge rode the Toddle-Bike to be like Peter.

CHAPTER 9   JUST ANOTHER RAINY DAY

I forgot all about Fudge and **concentrated** on the movie. It was much better than I thought it would be.

23. Which word means the same as **concentrated**?

   A. Focus attention

   B. Ignore

   C. Cluster together

CHAPTER 10   DRIBBLE

If the medicine didn't work soon, Fudge might have to have an operation. Things were pretty **dreary**.

24. Which means the same as **dreary**? (2 answers)

   A. Encouraging

   B. Unpleasant

   C. Interesting

   D. Sadness and gloom

25. What is the **problem** in this chapter?

    A. There was a chair in the middle of the doorway.

    B. Dribble was gone.

    C. Mr. Hatcher made an awful omelet.

26. Why did Peter name his dog Turtle?

    A. To remind him of the pet that died.

    B. He was miserable.

    C. Grandma told him what to name it.

THE WHIPPING BOY

By   Sid Fleischman

A bratty prince and his whipping boy have many adventures when they inadvertently trade places.

CHAPTER 1

1. When the guests stood up to toast the king, **why** did their wigs come flying off?

    A. Because the king was furious with them

    B. Because Prince Brat tied their wigs to the backs of their chairs

    C. Because the whipping boy and the prince were playing a game

The prince lowered his head so as to appear humbled and **contrite**.

2. What does the word **contrite** mean in this sentence?

    A. Showing no sense of guilt

    B. Apologetic, deeply sorry for having done wrong

    C. Uncaring

CHAPTER 2

3. How was the whipping boy **different** from the prince?

    A. He learned to read and write.

    B. He could not write his name.

    C. His tongue hangs out like a red flag.

CHAPTER 3

"I'm running away." The whipping boy sat **bolt** upright.

4. What does the word **bolt** mean in this sentence?

    A. A pin or rod for holding something in place

    B. A stroke of lightning

    C. To move suddenly

    D. A roll of cloth or wallpaper

5. Why did the prince want to run away?

   A. He was bored.

   B. He was angry at the king.

   C. He wanted more friends.

CHAPTER 4

The night moon had *lit their way like a lantern*.

6. What does this mean?

   A. It was very dark.

   B. The moon provided light so they could see their way.

   C. A thick fog had swirled in.

7. What happened to the prince and the whipping boy?

   A. They were captured by two outlaws.

   B. They found a new home.

   C. They became best friends.

"Take your hands off me, you **insolent** rascal!"

8. What does **insolent** mean in this sentence?   Polite   or   Disrespectful

CHAPTER 5

9. What did the big outlaw, Billy, smell like?

    A. Rotten eggs

    B. Sewer rats

    C. Garlic

The heir to the throne raised himself to his full height. "**Bow** to your prince!"

10. What does **bow** mean in this sentence?

    A. The forward part of a ship or boat

    B. A knot with loops in it

    C. To bend the head or body as in a greeting, worship, or saying yes

    D. To acknowledge applause of an audience

CHAPTER 6

The big man lifted out a golden **crown**. "That's mine!" bleated the prince.

11. What does the word **crown** mean in this sentence?

    A. The part of a tooth covered with enamel, outside the gum

    B. An ornament often set with jewels worn on the head as a sigh of power

    C. A British coin

    D. In checkers, to make a piece a king by placing another piece upon it

CHAPTER 7

"This ignorant whipping boy knows the letters---and the royal prince can't sign his own name. Something's **amiss** here," said Hold-Your-Nose Billy.

12. What is the meaning of the word **amiss**?

   A. Wrong, out of order
   B. Missing
   C. Rightly, correct

13. Why did Prince Brat's face turn *red as hot iron*?

   A. Because it was very hot in the hut
   B. Because the outlaws' thought Jemmy was the prince instead of him
   C. Because he could not breathe

CHAPTER 8

Prince Brat glared icily at the whipping boy who had **seized** his royal title.

14. What does **seized** mean in this sentence?

   A. Taken advantage of an opportunity
   B. Take hold of by force
   C. Released

CHAPTER 9

Jemmy sat on the bed of straw beside the prince and **contemplated** his breakfast. He examined the bread closely looking for varmints.

15. What does **contemplated** mean in this sentence?

    A. To think fully or deeply about
    B. To look at or view with attention; to observe thoroughly
    C. To disregard

16. What was Jemmy's **plan** to trick the villains?

    A. Poison the garlic.
    B. Write a hidden message within the ransom note to the king.
    C. Have the prince deliver the ransom note to the castle.

CHAPTER 10

Prince Brat hadn't shown a moment's interest in Jemmy's **scheme** to fee him.

17. Which word means the **same** as **scheme** in this sentence?

    A. An underhand plot or plan
    B. A diagram or map
    C. Any disorganization

"**Simpleton**! I swear there are not two more ignorant, cloven-footed blockheads in the land," said Jemmy.

18. Which **2 clues** in the sentence give **evidence** of the meaning of **simpleton**?

   A. Swear

   B. Ignorant

   C. Cloven-footed

   D. blockhead

"No," replied the prince flatly. He remained **defiant**. "I'm staying."

19. What does the word **defiant** mean in this sentence?

   A. Bold resistance to authority

   B. A challenge to engage in combat

   C. Submission

CHAPTER 11

20. What is the **problem** in this chapter?

   A. Hold-Your-Nose Billy needed more garlic.

   B. Jemmy wanted a share of the reward.

   C. Prince Brat refused to take the note to the castle.

21. What was the **solution** to the difficulty in this chapter?

    A. Let the horse carry the message back to the castle.

    B. The outlaws would share a bucket full of gold and jewels.

    C. The prince agreed to return home to his father.

CHAPTER 12

22. How did Prince Brat **betray** Jemmy?

    A. He promised Jemmy protection from the king.

    B. He told Cutwater where Jemmy was hiding.

    C. He tied Jemmy's hands behind his back.

CHAPTER 13

Jemmy turned to the right and beat his way back into the **foliage**.

23. What does **foliage** mean?

    A. The leaves on a tree or other plants

    B. Upturned hollow tree

    C. A castle

CHAPTER 14

The forest trees **rose** all around them *like prison bars.*

24. What is the **correct** meaning of **rose** in this sentence?

   A. A group of shrubs having thorny stems and fragrant flowers

   B. Appearance above the horizon

   C. To get up from sitting, lying or kneeling to an upright position

25. How was the forest **like** prison bars?

   A. They could not escape or find the way out. They were surrounded by trees.

   B. The outlaws held them prisoner.

   C. The bear had them cornered behind a tree.

CHAPTER 15

26. Why did the boys want to **collect** driftwood?

   A. To build a fire

   B. To cook their food

   C. To sell as firewood

27. What does the word **collect** mean in this sentence?

   A. To receive payment of

   B. To gather together or assemble

   C. To scatter

CHAPTER 16

"He must have a **hide** like an elephant," said Cutwater. "He don't feel a thing."

28. Which is the **correct** meaning of the word **hide** in this sentence?

   A. To put or keep out of sight; conceal
   B. the skin of an animal, especially when stripped from its carass
   C. the human skin
   D. reveal

CHAPTER 17

29. Why did Jemmy **change** his mind about the prince?

   A. He was amazed that Prince Brat didn't cry during his whipping.
   B. He was brave enough to pet Petunia the Bear.
   C. They both needed spectacles.

"You should have yelled and **bellowed**. That's what they wanted to hear."

30. What is the meaning of **bellowed**?

   A. Whispered
   B. To utter in a loud voice
   C. A loud animal cry as a bull or cow

CHAPTER 18

Jemmy never regarded fetching and carrying as a **privilege**.

31. What does the word **privilege** mean in this sentence?

    A. special benefit, favor, or advantage

    B. responsibility

    C. misfortune

32. What **two** things **did** Prince Brat **experience** for the first time?

    A. He had never shaken hands.

    B. He had never milked a cow.

    C. He had never eaten a potato.

CHAPTER 19

Jemmy didn't wait to be spotted. But it was to late. The big outlaw gave a distant yell and **altered** his course.

33. Which word means the **same** as **altered**?

    A. Continued

    B. Changed

    C. Carried

The prince's voice was almost **inaudible**. "What's to the left?"

34. What is the meaning of the word **inaudible**?

    A. Not loud, soundless

    B. Booming, shouting

    C. Loud enough to be heard

They could make a run for the river. But in his sudden **elation**, Jemmy banged into the wall with the birdcage.

35. Which word means the **same** as **elation** in this sentence?

    A. Unhappiness

    B. Joyfulness

    C. Fear

36. Why did the outlaws look *like they were wearing fur coats?*

    A. Their beards had grown over three feet.

    B. The mud from the sewer was smeared all over them.

    C. Rats were swarming and clinging to the two of them.

CHAPTER 20

Jemmy gave the prince a blazing look. The prince returned a quick playful wink. He saw for the first time the prince was up to a kindly piece of **mischief**.

37. What does the word **mischief** mean in this sentence?

　A. Conduct or activity that playfully causes annoyance

　B. Injury or evil caused by a person

　C. Bad or wrong chief

38. What happened to Jemmy when he returned to the castle?

　A. The king ordered him to be whipped.

　B. He was placed under the protection of the prince.

　C. He decided to run away.

"You got me off without so much as a single whack," Jemmy whispered.

"I couldn't **bear** all the yowling and bellowing." Said Prince Brat.

39. What is the meaning of the word **bear** in this sentence?

　A. A large, very strong mammal with a furry body and short tail

　B. To hold up, support

　C. To endure or tolerate

DONAVAN'S WORD JAR

By   Monalisa DeGross

When the jar that Donavan keeps his word collection in fills up, he finds a special way to give his words away and get something wonderful in return.

CHAPTER 1   DONAVAN

Like most of the kids in his class, Donavan liked to **collect** things.

1. Which meaning is correct for the word **collect** in this sentence?

    A. To receive a payment of

    B. To accumulate

    C. To scatter

CHAPTER 2   DONAVAN'S DISCOVERY

2. What important thing did Donavan **discover** in this chapter?

    A. New words are everywhere, and he liked finding them.

    B. He found a new tool in his father's tool chest that looked like a crab claw.

    C. It was better to write the words in purple ink on yellow sheets of paper.

3. Why did Donavan decide to keep his word jar high up on the shelf in his room?

    A. Because he didn't want his sister snooping around it

    B. Because collecting words was fun

    C. Because the word jar was jam-packed

CHAPTER 3   DONAVAN'S DILEMMA

4. What is Donavan's **problem** in this chapter?

    A. Mom punished him because he didn't eat the raw vegetables in his lunch.

    B. He is concerned that he didn't know how to start his own dictionary.

    C. There isn't space for another word in his word jar.

"Dad, that idea would take too long," Donavan said **impatiently**." Can't you think of something I can do right now?"

5. Which means the **same** as **impatiently** in this sentence?

    A. Violently

    B. Very eager

    C. Angrily

CHAPTER 4   DONAVAN'S DECISION

6. What was Donavan's **decision** in this chapter?

    A. He wanted to see his grandmother to ask for ideas about his problem.

    B. He wanted to stay awake all night and look at the words in the word jar.

    C. He wanted to be a good big brother and sit with his sick sister.

"Your father is down in the basement working on the **sign** for his shop. He can't have any **interruptions**. He needs peace and quiet so that he can **concentrate**," Donavan's mom said firmly.

7. Which is the **correct** meaning of the word **sign** in this context?

    A. A signal or hint

    B. A board with information or advertisement posted for public view

    C. To write a signature

    D. A mathematical symbol such as plus for addition, minus for subtraction

8. What is the meaning for **interruptions** in this sentence?

    A. Disturbance

    B. Help or assistance

    C. Agreement

9. Which words mean the **same** as **concentrate** in this sentence?

    A. To ignore and forget

    B. To disregard and neglect

    C. To focus and give attention

CHAPTER 5 DONAVAN'S DELAY

10. Why was Nikki feeling better at the **end** of this chapter?

    A. Because Donavan performed magic tricks for her

    B. Because the words cheered her up and made her laugh

    C. Because Donavan watched cartoons with her

CHAPTER 6 DONAVAN'S DEPARTURE

Ask your Grandma if she's **free** to come to dinner tonight?

11. Which is the **correct** meaning of the word **free** as used in this sentence?

    A. A person who is not in slavery or imprisonment

    B. Able to do something, unoccupied, not busy

    C. Clear of obstructions or obstacles

    D. Provided without charge or fee

CHAPTER 7   DONAVAN DINES

12. What was the **best** thing about Grandma's new apartment?

    A. Donavan could visit her often because she only lived a few blocks away.

    B. She lived on the fourth floor in the senior citizens apartment building.

    C. The picture hall had a picture of his grandpop.

CHAPTER 8   DONAVAN'S DISAPPOINTMENT

13. What is Donovan's **disappointment** in this chapter?

    A. He did not like Grandma's solution to his problem.

    B. Kids did not play with a kaleidoscope anymore.

    C. The word collection was soaking wet from the rain.

CHAPTER 9   DONAVAN'S DIPLOMACY

14. How did the word COMPROMISE effectively solve the problem?

   A. Miz Marylou giggled, and Mr. Bill Gut smiled.

   B. Miz Marylou and Mr. Bill were talking quietly and coming to an agreement.

   C. No one in the room were looking at each other.

CHAPTER 10   DONAVAN'S DELIGHT

15. Why was Donavan **delighted** at the **end** of this chapter? (2 answers)

   A. He would be proud to put his new collection of words in his grandpop's jar.

   B. Grandma was worried because her neighbors did not give him anything for the words.

   C. Donavan's words changed the neighbors. They were no longer unhappy but were up laughing and talking.

   D. Donavan waited while Grandma got her coat and locked the apartment.

CODE 7 CRACKING THE CODE FOR AN EPIC LIFE

by   Bryan R. Johnson

Life at Flint Hill Elementary School may seem normal, but seven friends soon find themselves on a path to crack the code for an epic life.

1   A WORLD OF POSSIBILITIES

"They're going to tear this place down!" said Darren. Jefferson knew they'd never **demolish** the school.

1. What does the word **demolish** mean in this sentence?

    A. rebuild or construct

    B. To destroy, ruin, wreck, bulldoze

    C. To repair and mend

Jefferson thought about Flint Hill Elementary, sitting atop its grassy, **manicured** slope.

2. What does the word **manicured** mean in this sentence?

    A. A cosmetic treatment of the fingernails, removing cuticles

    B. To use concrete and rocks to beautify

    C. To cut and trim with extreme and precise care

"I can't wait to see your **vision** for the mural," said Principal Cooler.

3. Which is the meaning of **vision** in this sentence?

    A. Concept or idea

    B. eyesight

After the feedback from the audience, Jefferson had to come up with a **revision**.

4. Which means the **same** as **revision** in this sentence?

    A. Accusations

    B. Changes

    C. Contact lens

5. What was the **problem** after Jefferson presented the image of the teachers' ideas?

    A. All the teachers wanted a cup of coffee.

    B. They wanted the books arranged by the Dewey Decimal system.

    C. Many of the students were upset that their ideas were not included.

6. What did Mr. Summers, the groundskeeper, suggest to Jefferson?

   A. Paint the mural on the wall and then ask what everyone thinks.

   B. Tell the principal to find a professional to paint the mural.

   C. To help him with the broken lawn mower.

2   SMASH MOUTH TAFFY

7. What was Great-Aunt Martha's **idea** for Sebastian to have the latest gaming system?

   A. To do something worthwhile like soccer

   B. Do chores and earn the money to buy the system

   C. Think of something else to buy

He went to the bedroom to **sulk** about how unreasonable the ideas were.

8. Which word means the **opposite** of **sulk**?

   A. Smile

   B. Mope

   C. Frown

Sebastian got up and **nudged** his brother out of his room.

9. Which word means the **same** as **nudged**?

    A. A gentle push

    B. Pinched

    C. Manipulated

He unwrapped it and the **scent** of taffy filled the air.

10. What is the meaning of the word **scent** in this sentence?

    A. To hunt with a sense of smell as a hound

    B. A distinctive odor

    C. Bouquet

By his **calculations**, he could make at least one batch of taffy per night.

11. What is the meaning of the word **calculations** in this sentence?

    A. Estimation and prediction

    B. Adding, subtracting, multiplying, and dividing

    C. Computations

Smash Mouth Taffy soon *caught on like wildfire* in the halls of school.

12. What does this phrase *caught on like wildfire* mean?

    A. The hallways of the school was on fire.

    B. The taffy sold very quickly.

    C. Extra baggies, sugar, and sticks of butter disappeared.

"Cooties!" Someone said dramatically. **Pandemonium** broke out in the cafeteria.

13. What is the meaning of **pandemonium** in this sentence?

    A. Chaos and disorder

    B. Peace and harmony

    C. Silence; no talking zone

14. Which **text evidence** gives a **clue** to the meaning of **pandemonium**?

    A. The girl began to scratch at her arm.

    B. Everyone jumped up from the tables to get away.

    C. There was a food fight in the cafeteria.

15. Why was Sebastian in the principal's office?

    A. Because he knew that stealing money was a bad idea.

    B. Because more than a hundred people wanted to buy more taffy.

    C. Because every single hive-infested student had purchased his candy.

3   HANDLE WITH CARE

16. What **project** did Miss Skeen give the class for a week?

    A. To hatch a real chicken from an egg

    B. To practice frying eggs with creative recipes

    C. To take care of an egg for seven days

17. What is the **purpose** of the project?

    A. To learn what its like to care for something or someone

    B. To learn about the life cycle of an egg and chicken

    C. To get rid of the abundance of eggs from the cafeteria

Take the egg wherever you go and **record** your experiences.

18. Which is the **correct** meaning for **record** as used in this sentence?

   A. The best achievement in some sports

   B. A disc where sound is store and played on a phonograph

   C. To write down specific information

4   THE MONSTER

He adjusted his baseball cap and **cast** his line. He was going to catch the big fish.

19. Which is the **correct** meaning for the word **cast** as used in this sentence?

   A. To select actors for a play or movie

   B. To throw or hurl with force, to sling

   C. Something shaped or formed into a mold

20. What is central **message** or life **lesson** of this chapter?

   A. Determination and perseverance

   B. Honest and integrity

   C. Always do your homework

5   BREAK A LEG

21. Why was Samantha in the drama club?

   A. She wanted to wear a feather boa over her shoulder.

   B. She loved theater and everything about it.

   C. She wanted to learn to sing.

Trista was **mediocre**. She couldn't remember her lines.

22. What is the **opposite** meaning of **mediocre**? (3 answers)

   A. Excellent

   B. Barely adequate

   C. Not satisfactory

   D. Extraordinary

   E. Commonplace

   F. Superior

   G. Inferior

6   OH RATS!

The **stench** of the rotting bananas began to mix in with the odor of moldy cheese.

23. What is the meaning of the word **stench** in this sentence?

    A. Offensive odor

    B. Sweetness

    C. Perfumed scent

24. Why did Alec finally decide to clean his room?

    A. A giant-sized rat was gnawing through his pillowcase.

    B. He wanted better for his baby sister's future.

    C. A siren went off and six men in protective suits invaded his room.

25. What life **lesson** did Alec learn?

    A. There are consequences for keeping a dirty room.

    B. Mothers do not clean a fifth grader's room.

    C. Get back on the horse and try again.

CODE 7

After everyone had voted, it was **unanimous** to submit Kaitlyn's project.

26. What is the meaning of **unanimous**?

   A. Split decision

   B. Complete agreement

   C. Unacceptable

27. How did Kaitlyn **change** from the beginning of the chapter?

   A. She was no longer alone and lonely.

   B. She lost interest in filming.

   C. She wanted a new messenger bag.

CHARLOTTE'S WEB

by E. B. White

A little girl and Charlotte, a beautiful grey spider, struggle to save Wilbur the pig from being butchered.

CHAPTER I   BEFORE BREAKFAST

"Well," said her mother, "one of the pigs is a **runt.** It's very small and weak; and it will never amount to anything. So, your father has decided to do away with it."

1. What is the meaning of the word **runt?**

    A. An old cow or ox

    B. An old or decayed tree stump

    C. The smallest or weakest of a litter, especially of puppies or piglets.

"Do away with it?" **shrieked** Fern.

2. What is the meaning of the word **shrieked?**

   A. A loud, high sound of laughter

   B. To cry out sharply in a high voice

   C. To sound of a whistle

3. Which word means the **same** as **shrieked?**

   A. Yell

   B. Kill it

   C. Amount

Mrs. Arable put a **pitcher** of cream on the table.

4. What is the correct meaning of the word, **pitcher** as used in this sentence?

   A. A visual representation of a person, object, or scene as a painting, drawing, or photograph

   B. A container, usually with a handle and spout, for holding or pouring liquids

   C. A part of a plant

"But it's **unfair**," cried Fern

5. The prefix **un—** helps the reader understand that **unfair** means.

    A. Without fair

    B. Not fair

    C. Really fair

"I see no difference," replied Fern, still hanging on to the ax. "This is the most terrible case of **injustice** I ever heard of."

6. Which word is an **antonym**, or the **opposite**, of the word **injustice**?

    A. Wrong

    B. Kindness

    C. injury

7. Which word is a **synonym**, means the **same**, as the word **injustice**?

    A. Wrong

    B. Kindness

    C. Injury

"Can I have a pig, too, Pop?" asked Avery. "No, I only **distribute** pigs to early risers," said Mr. Arable.

8. What does the word **distribute** mean in this context?

    A. To promote, sell, and ship

    B. To pass out or deliver to intended recipients

9. How is the **problem** finally solved?

    A. Fern's brother shot the pig with his rifle.

    B. Fern's father allowed her to keep the pig.

    C. Fern's mother yelled at her husband to kill the pig.

10. Which **clue** shows that the **setting,** where this takes place, is in the past?

    A. The kitchen table was set for breakfast.

    B. The school bus honked from the road.

    C. The room smelled of wood smoke from the stove.

CHAPTER II   WILBUR

11. Why did Mr. Arable fix a small yard for Wilbur under an apple tree?

    A. Because he fell down the stairs.

    B. Because after two weeks, he was moved outdoors.

    C. Because Fern spilled milk on the floor of the kitchen.

Fern went down to the brook for a swim. Wilbur **tagged** along at Fern's heels.

12. What is the correct meaning of the word **tagged** in this sentence?

    A. To write graffiti

    B. To follow closely; to go about as a follower

    C. To furnish with a tag, such as a cow

13. Why was Wilbur moved to the Zuckerman's barn at five weeks old?

    A. Because Mr. Arable said Wilbur had to be sold

    B. Because Wilbur was born in the springtime

    C. Because Wilbur wanted to live in a manure pile

CHAPTER III   ESCAPE

The goose said, "Go down through the orchard and **root** up the sod!"

14. What is the correct meaning of the word **root** as used in this sentence?

    A. To cheer and shout encouragement

    B. The part of a plant that grows into the earth

    C. To turn up or dig with the snout

Mrs. Zuckerman saw Wilbur from the kitchen window and immediately shouted for the men. "Homer! Pig's out!" The goose heard the **racket** and she too started hollering. The cocker spaniel heard the commotion, and he ran out from the barn to join the chase.

15. What does the word **racket** mean in this context?

    A. A light bat used in tennis and badminton consisting of a handle attached to an oval frame

    B. Loud noise, clatter, or commotion

    C. A dishonest method or scheme of getting money or goods

16. When he looked up and saw Mr. Zuckerman holding a pan of warm slops, Wilbur felt **relieved**. Why?

      A. Because Lurvy fetched a hammer and nails to fix the fence

      B. The food smelled appetizing.

      C. Fern was there to comfort him.

CHAPTER IV LONELINESS

17. Which **character** did Wilbur plan to have a talk with from seven to eight?

      A. Avery, Fern's brother

      B. Templeton, the rat

      C. The cocker spaniel

"Play?" said Templeton. "I hardly know the meaning of the word." "It means to have fun, to **frolic**, to run and to skip and to make merry, " said Wilbur.

18. What is the **antonym**, or **opposite** meaning, of the word **frolic**?

      A. Playful behavior

      B. Sleepy

      C. Afraid

CHAPTER V   CHARLOTTE

Wilbur heard Templeton **gnawing** a hole in the grain bin. His teeth scraped loudly against the wood. "Why does he have to stay up all night, grinding his clashers and destroying people's property?" asked Wilbur.

19. What is the meaning of the word **gnawing** ?

    A. Commotion

    B. Biting or nibbling

20. Which word is a **synonym**, or means the **same**, for **gnawing**?

    A. Property

    B. Grinding

"First," said Charlotte, "I dive at him." She **plunged** headfirst towards the fly. As she dropped, a tiny silken thread unwound from her rear end.

21. Which word means the **same** as **plunged** in this sentence?

    A. First
    B. Unwound
    C. Dropped

"All of us spiders have had to work the same trick of spinning a web. It's not a bad **pitch** on the whole," said Charlotte.

22. What is the **correct** meaning of the word **pitch** as used in this sentence?

   A. To throw toss or hurl

   B. The level of a sound's highness or lowness

   C. To erect or set up

23. What **would happen** if spiders did **not** catch and eat bugs?

   A. Spiders would lose their inheritance.

   B. Bugs would increase and multiple and get so numerous.

   C. The goose eggs would not receive heat.

CHAPTER VI   SUMMER DAYS

With her broad **bill** the goose pushed the unhatched egg out of the nest, and the entire company watched in disgust while the rat rolled it away.

24. What is the **correct** meaning of the word **bill** as used in this context?

   A. A statement of money owed for work done or things supplied.

   B. A piece of paper money

   C. A proposed law offered to a legislative body

   D. The mouth part of a bird

   E. The program of a theatrical performance

CHAPTER VII   BAD NEWS

Flies spent their time **pestering** others. The cows hated them. The horses detested them. The sheep loathed them. Mr. and Mrs. Zuckerman were always complaining about them.

25. What does the word **pestering** mean in this sentence?

    A. To bother persistently with petty annoyances

    B. To overcrowd

    C. Helpful

CHAPTER   VIII   A TALK AT HOME

" I worry about Fern," said Mrs. Arable. "Did you hear the way she **rambled** on about the animals, pretending that they talked?"

26. What does **ramble** mean in the context of this sentence?

    A.   To wander around in an aimless manner

    B. To talk aimlessly on and on

CHAPTER IX   WILBUR'S BOAST

A spider's web is stronger than it looks. Although it is made of thin **delicate** strands, the web is not easily broken.

27. Which **clue** from the context shows that **delicate** means weak and fragile?

    A. Easily broken

    B. Thin

    C. Web

"Got a little piece of string I could borrow?" asked Wilbur. " Yes indeed," replied Templeton, who saved string. "No trouble at all. Anything to **oblige**."

28. What does the word **oblige** mean in this sentence?

    A. To do a favor for or service for

    B. To force or bind, as in to follow the law

"I could spin a web if I tried," said Wilbur **boasting**. "I just never tried."

29. What does the word **boast** mean?

    A. A bragging statement

    B. To shape roughly with a chisel

    C. To cry constantly

CHAPTER X   AN EXPLOSION

"I was just thinking," said the spider, "that people are very **gullible**."

30. What clues on this page in the novel help to determine the meaning of the word **gullible?**

    Easy to fool   or   Affectionately

"Come on frog!" cried Avery. He scooped up his frog. The frog kicked, splashing soapy water onto the blueberry pie. "Another **crisis**!" groaned Fern.

31. Which word means the **opposite** of **crisis**?

    A. Disaster

    B. Good fortune

32. What **caused** the explosion?

  A. The rotten egg broke.

  B. Avery knocked the spider into the box.

  C. The animals came up from the pasture.

CHAPTER XI   THE MIRACLE

A look of complete **bewilderment** came over Mrs. Zuckerman's face. "Homer Zuckerman, what in the world are you talking about?" she said.

33. What is the meaning of **bewilderment** in this sentence?

  A. Confusion

  B. Wilder

  C. Anger

34. What is Fern's **problem** at the **end** of this chapter?

  A. Mrs. Zuckerman failed to put up blackberry jam.

  B. Mrs. Arable sent Avery to bed without any supper.

  C. The barn was not nearly as pleasant—too many people.

CHAPTER XI   A MEETING

"Well, we are all here except the rat," said Charlotte. "I guess we can **proceed** without him."

35. What is the meaning of the word **proceed** in this sentence?

   A. To continue

   B. To discontinue or stop

   C. The profits from a sale or investment

36. What was the **purpose** of the meeting?

   A. To find someone to help Charlotte weave the words in the web.

   B. To get suggestions and ideas for words in the web.

   C. To convince Templeton the rat to help.

CHAPTER XIII   GOOD PROGRESS

"My cousin wrapped the fish up so tight it couldn't **budge**," said Charlotte.

37. What is the meaning of the word **budge**?

   A. Move

   B. Change one's mind

   C. Persuade someone

CHAPTER XIV DR. DORIAN

38. Why did Mrs. Arable visit the doctor?

     A. Because she had a stomachache

     B. Because she was concerned about Fern

     C. Because she was worried about Avery

CHAPTER XV THE CRICKETS

Some of Wilbur's friends in the barn worried the attention would make him stuck up. But it never did. Wilbur was **modest**; fame did not spoil him.

39. Which word means the **opposite** of **modest**?

     A. Boastful

     B. Humble

     C. Bashful

"The Fair comes at a bad time for me. I shall find it **inconvenien**t to leave home."

40. Which word means the **same** as **inconvenient**?

    A. Okay

    B. Bothersome

    C. Helpful

CHAPTER XVI OFF TO THE FAIR

A fair is a rat's paradise. A rat can creep out at night and enjoy a feast. "Is this appetizing **yarn** of yours true?" he asked.

41. What does **yarn** mean in this sentence?

    A. Any spun strand, natural or synthetic, used in weaving or knitting

    B. An adventure story, usually one that is made up

42. Mrs. Zuckerman decided to give Wilbur a bath in what?

    A. Buttermilk
    B. Oatmeal
    C. Blackberry jam

CHAPTER XVII UNCLE

"And don't **cross** the racetrack when the horses are coming!"

43. Which is the **correct** meaning of the word **cross** in this sentence?

    A. To draw a line across

    B. Two intersecting lines

    C. To move or pass from one side to the other side of

    D. Bad-tempered

One thing is certain, he has a most unattractive personality. He is too noisy, and he cracks **weak** jokes.

44. What is the meaning of the word **weak** in this context?

    A. Breakable

    B. Seven days

    C. Lacking in creative effectiveness

CHAPTER XVIII THE COOL OF THE EVENING

Templeton's keen nose **detected** many fine smells in the air.

45. What is the meaning of the word **detected** in this sentence?

    A. Did not understand

    B. Identify and recognize

He **vanished** into the shadows.

46. What is the meaning of the word **vanished**?

    A. He decided to leave

    B. Satisfied

    C. Fetching and carrying

CHAPTER XIX THE EGG SAC

"It's a perfectly beautiful egg sac," said Wilbur, feeling as happy as though he had **constructed** it himself.

47. What is the **correct** meaning of the word, **constructed** in this sentence?

    A. Destroy or dismantle

    B. Build or form

    C. To draw

48. Why does Charlotte feel **downhearted** in this chapter?

    A. The rat was swollen to twice his size.

    B. The pig next door, called Uncle, had won first prize.

    C. She was sad because she wouldn't ever see her children.

CHAPTER XX   THE HOUR OF TRIUMPH

49. What was the hour of triumph?

    A. Wilbur was given a special award.

    B. Henry invited Fern to ride the Ferris wheel again.

    C. Charlotte could hear everything that was said on the loudspeaker.

50. **After** reading this chapter, what do you think the word **triumph** means?

    A. Unhappiness

    B. To achieve victory or success

CHAPTER XXI   LAST DAY

Wilbur was **desperate**. The people were coming. And the rat was failing him.

51. What is the meaning of the word **desperate**?

    A. Having an urgent need

    B. Hopeful

    C. Cowardly

52. Why did Templeton the Rat decide to help Wilbur?

    A. Because they were best friends

    B. Because he would eat first from the food trough each day

    C. Because it was the last day of the fair

CHAPTER XXII   A WARM WIND

Wilbur was **frantic**. Charlotte's babies were disappearing at a great rate.

53. How was Wilbur **feeling**?

    A. Peaceful and calm

    B. Distraught and fearful

    C. Pleased

54. Fern did **not** come regularly to the barn anymore. **Why not**?

   A. Because she was growing up and avoided childish things

   B. Because she developed a fear of spiders

   C. Because she married Henry and moved away

Wilbur never forgot Charlotte. Although he loved her children and grandchildren dearly, none of the new spiders ever took her place in his heart. She was in a **class** by herself.

55. What is the **correct** meaning of **class** as used in this **context**?

   A. A meeting of a group of students for instruction

   B. To group or categorize, rank

   C. Sharing a similar social position or economic status, such as middle class

   D. Excellence; exceptional

THE CHOCOLATE TOUCH

By   Patrick Skene Catling

Instead of gold, everything John Midas touched turned to precious chocolate.

1

John had one bad **fault**: he was a pig about candy, above all, chocolates. He **devoured** them all.

1. What is the **correct** meaning of the word **fault** in this sentence?

    A. A break in the earth's crust causing rock layers to shift

    B. Something that makes a person or thing less than perfect

    C. A mistake or blunder

2. Which word means the **same** as **devoured** in this sentence?

    A. To swallow or eat hungrily

    B. Nibble

    C. Dislike

An upset stomach can lead to all sorts of **complications**.

3. Which **two** words mean the **same** as **complications**?

    A. Problems

    B. satisfaction

    C. Simplicity

    D. Obstacles

2

4. Why was John deeply **disappointed** at the **end** of this chapter?

    A. Because the whole box only had one piece of chocolate.

    B. Because the tonic tasted like mud, glue, ink, and paint.

    C. Because he did not get a chance to play with Susan all afternoon.

3

5. What did John do **before** he put the orange juice to is lips?

    A. He pretended to eat the toothpaste.

    B. He scraped up a small piece of egg and put it into his mouth.

    C. He put the end of the toothpaste tube into is mouth and emptied it onto his tongue.

4

6. What is the **problem** at the **end** of this chapter?

    A. John ate a portion of Susan's silver dollar.

    B. Tears trickled down Susan's cheeks like rain down a windowpane.

    C. John's face was red with embarrassment.

5

John tried to write with his changed pencil, but the **point** was soft.

7. Which is the correct meaning for the word **point** in this sentence?

    A. To direct or aim, as a finger or weapon

    B. The sharp or tapered end of something

    C. A punctuation mark, especially a period

6

8. What is the **main problem** in this chapter?

    A. John messed up the arithmetic test.

    B. John was sad about Susan's anger and disbelief.

    C. Everything John put into his mouth changed to chocolate.

    D. John was afraid his mother would be upset about the missing gloves.

Every solid and liquid that he sampled was **transformed** as it entered his mouth.

9. Which word means the **same** as **transformed?**

    A. Kept

    B. Converted

    C. Polished

John's tray was loaded with just the sort of meal his mother was always trying to **persuade** him to eat.

10. What is the meaning of the word **persuade**?

    A. Influence

    B. Discourage

    C. Provide for

With her **baton**, Mrs. Quaver rapped twice sharply on the music stand before her.

11. Which is the **correct** meaning for **baton** in this sentence?

    A. A wand used by a conductor

    B. A lightweight rod twirled by a majorette

    C. A plastic or hollow rod that is passed during a race

Susan poised her **bow** over the strings of the violin.

12. Which is the **correct** meaning of **bow** for this sentence?

    A. To bend the head or body in a greeting

    B. The forward part of a ship

    C. A knot with loops in it

    D. A rod used to play an instrument

Susan and John immediately pulled their heads up and their faces were **drenched** in chocolate syrup.

13. Which is the **correct** meaning for **drenched** in this sentence?

    A. To wet thoroughly, soaked

    B. A large drink

    C. Mixture of pesticide and water applied to the soil

10

John choked and chocolate syrup spurted from his mouth. Dr. Cranium dropped the spoon in **alarm**.

14. Which is the **correct** meaning for the word **alarm** in this sentence?

    A. Any signal or sound used to warn others of danger

    B. A device, such as a bell or siren, used to give a signal

    C. A sudden feeling of fear, apprehension, distress, or panic

    D. Encouragement and calmness

15. Why did John run wildly out of the house?

    A. Because his mother had turned into a lifeless statue of chocolate.

    B. Because he couldn't bear to see his mother's tears.

    C. Because Mr. Midas blew his nose and abruptly left the room.

The **proprietor** must know a lot about John's hateful chocolate touch. John rushed into the store.

16. What is the meaning of the word p**roprietor**?

    A. Customer

    B. Business owner

    C. Exclusive title to something

17. What (3) **lessons** did John learn?

    A. Unselfishness and honesty are important

    B. He could work in the store for nothing to have his mother back.

    C. He had only himself to blame for all his unhappiness.

    D. Chocolatitis is not curable

    E. Be concerned about other people

12

John ran **briskly** down the street until he came to the corner.

18. Which word means the **same** as **briskly**?

    A. Slowly

    B. Sluggishly

    C. Energetically

    D. Angrily

SOPHIA WASHINGTON: QUEEN OF THE BEE

by   Tonya Duncan Ellis

If there is one thing 10-year-old Texan Sophie Washington is good at, it's spelling. She's earned straight 100s on all her spelling tests to prove it. Her parents want her to compete in the Xavier Academy spelling bee.

CHAPTER 1   THREE LITTLE PIGS

1. Wy did the wild boar dig up the lawn?

    A. To look for grubs and bugs to eat

    B. Bo splash in the rain puddles and mud

    C. To help Dad with replanting the grass

CHAPTER 2   MUTTON BUSTIN

"If you two don't stop **bickering**, we're heading home," Mom warns.

2. Which word means the **same** as **bickering** in this sentence?

    A. Quarreling or controversy

    B. A flickering light

    C. Making a rushing sound as water

CHAPTER 3   MR. KNOW-IT-ALL

3. Why is Nathan Jones secretly called Mr. Know-It-All?

    A. Because he won the spelling bee last year

    B. Because he thinks he knows the answer to everything

    C. Because he has the biggest mouth in fifth grade

CHAPTER 4   PRACTICE MAKES PERFECT

4. What is the **problem** in this chapter?

    A. Dad had to work late at his dental practice.

    B. Cole had a rock stuck in his ear.

    C. Cole broke something downstairs.

CHAPTER 5   A SMALL WORLD

5. How did the doctor remove the rock from Cole's ear?

    A. Use tweezers to get hold of the rock

    B. Tells him to lean his head to the side and the rocks fall out

    C. Fill his ear with water and the rocks float out

6. What makes it **"A Small World"** in this chapter?

   A. Because Sophie meets Nathan's mom, a nurse, at the doctor's office

   B. Because Sophie's mom is friends with Nathan's mom

   C. Because Xavier's Academy has a super cool logo on their sweaters

CHAPTER 6   THE BEAT DOWN

Nathan tries to play it off like he isn't scared, but he can tell Chloe is **serious**.

7. Which means the **same** as **serious** in this sentence?

   A. Crucial

   B. Determined

   C. Happy

CHAPTER 7   STUDY TIME

8. Which is Sophie's **best** way to study her spelling words?

    A. Write each word ten times

    B. Practice while jumping rope

    C. Memorizing the words

CHAPTER 8   GRANNY WASHINGTON

I smile with **contentment** as I drift off to sleep. Having grandparents visit is the best.

9. Which word means the **opposite** of <u>contentment</u> in this sentence?

    A. Pleasure and gladness

    B. Disappointment

    C. Satisfaction

    D. Happiness

CHAPTER 9   R-E-S-P-E-C-T

My heart **pounds** in my chest and my hands feel cold.

10. Which is the **correct** meaning for the word **pounds** in this sentence?

   A. A unit of weight equivalent to 16 ounces

   B. A place for keeping stray animals

   C. To beat or throb heavily

The school is **adjacent** to the gymnasium.

11. What is the meaning of the word **adjacent** in this sentence?

   A. Disconnected

   B. Adjoining, beside, or next to

   C. Distant and far away; divided

CHAPTER 10   OH BROTHER

12. Why does Sophie think that sometimes having a little brother is not so bad?

   A. Cole draws her a picture with "Congratulations Sophie!" on it.

   B. Cole is able to tune out everything around him when he's working.

   C. Listening to the brat is like music to her ears.

CHAPTER 11   FUN PLEX

We play air hockey, video games, and I have a **blast** on the bumper cars.

13. Which is the **correct** meaning for the word **blast** as used in this sentence?

   A. Loud sound

   B. Fun time

   C. Quiet

CHAPTER 12   GOLDY

14. Why did Dad think that Sophie **deserved** a reward?

   A. She agreed to go to a birthday party with her younger brother.

   B. She always help Mom with the housework.

   C. She proved that she was responsible.

CHAPTER 13   ODD GIRL OUT

15. What is the **main problem** in this chapter?

   A. With 21 students, it makes an odd person out when pairs are made.

   B. Chloe did not want to be a boy character.

   C. The new girl is sitting alone at her desk.

CHAPTER 14   AFRICAN QUEENS

Mariama's hair was covered with a cut pink scarf that had a swirly yellow and brown pattern on it and was tied in a **knot** in the front.

16. Which is the **correct** meaning for the word **knot** as used in this sentence?

    A. An ornamental bow of silk, lace, ribbon, braid, etc.

    B. A group of people as a crew, crowd, band or company

    C. A bond or union; a marriage

CHAPTER 15   BOUBOU AND BROCCOLI

This is one of the most **unique** costumes I've seen on Twin Day," says Mrs. Green.

17. Which is the **same** meaning as **unique** in this sentence?

    A. Incomparable

    B. Ordinary

    C. Normal

CHAPTER 16   SEE YOU LATER ALLIGATOR

18. Why were there alligators in their neighborhood?

   A. Alligators lived in the creeks long before the houses were built in the area.

   B. The subdivision allowed pet alligators in the neighborhood.

   C. They were trying to protect their babies from predators.

CHAPTER 17   REGIONALS

"Remember to keep your **focus** and stay calm while spelling each word."

19. Which is the **same** meaning of **focus** as used in this sentence?

   A. Blurry vision

   B. Attraction

   C. Aim attention at

CHAPTER 18   ROOM 105

20. Why is Sophie **nervous** about the wildcard list of words?

   A. Because the judge starts naming words that she's never heard in her life.

   B. Because the competitors begin to take seats in the back one by one.

   C. Because Nathan has studied the sixth-grade list of words.

CHAPTER 19   V-I-C-T-O-R-Y

21. What was so **special** for Sophie about being the winner of the regionals spelling bee?

   A. She won and Nathan did not.

   B. It had been years since someone from her school had won first place.

   C. Her nerves did not cause her to mess up.

CHAPTER 20   QUEEN OF THE BEE

22. Why did Sophie **not** compete in the spell down competition?

    A. She had already won a blue ribbon for first place.

    B. This was for winners in the sixth grade and up categories.

    C. She had forgotten to sign up to compete in this category.

23. What **decision** did Sophie make at the **end** of the novel?

    A. To stand in the center for each photo so that her medal was on display.

    B. To be nicer to Nathan even though he acts like a jerk a lot of the time.

    C. To wear the tiara every day to feel like a queen.

THE MOUSE AND THE MOTORCYCLE

By   Beverly Cleary

A reckless young mouse named Ralph makes friends with a boy in room 215 of the Mountain View Inn and discovers the joys of motorcycling.

CHAPTER 1   THE NEW GUESTS

1. Why did the family arrive at the Mountain View Inn?

    A. Because they were only twenty-five miles from Highway 40.

    B. Because Mr. Gridley needed a rest after four hundred miles of driving.

    C. Because the boy was feeling sick.

CHAPTER 2   THE MOTORCYCLE

At first, a young mouse named Ralph, was disappointed at the size of the boy who was to **occupy** the room.

2. What does the word **occupy** mean in this sentence ?

    A. To take or fill up space

    B. To be lazy, to reject

    C. To employ

The **momentum** of the motorcycle carried him over the edge of the table.

3. What is the meaning of the word **momentum**?

    A. Weakness

    B. Force of movement

    C. Charm or keepsake

4. What is the **problem** at the **end** of this chapter?

    A. Ralph fell in the metal wastebasket.

    B. Ralph scrabbled his feet on the tabletop.

    C. The bell on the telephone only rang half a ring.

CHAPTER 3   TRAPPED!

He should have been **content** to stay home without going out into the world.

5. Which is the **correct** meaning for **content** in this sentence?

    A. Something that is contained

    B. The subjects or topics covered in a book

    C. A feeling of happiness and satisfaction

    D. Something that is expressed through speech or writing

"Go away," said Ralph crossly, because it embarrassed him to be seen in such a **predicament**.

6. What is the meaning of the word **predicament**?

    A. in good fortune

    B. in a difficult or dangerous situation

    C. in a tug of war with ants

7. What happened **after** Ralph had eaten his fill of the apple?

    A. He was exhausted and fell asleep.

    B. He rolled the motorcycle over to the wall of the wastebasket.

    C. He jumped to his feet and leaped against the wall.

CHAPTER 4   KEITH

8. What does the boy ask Ralph **first**?

    A. How did you get up here in the first place?

    B. Are you asleep?

    C. How did you get in here?

    D. Are you getting ready for bed?

Lie low indeed! Ralph was **indignant**. He couldn't lie much lower if he wanted to.

9. What is the meaning of **indignant** in this sentence?

    A. Expressing strong displeasure of something; insulting

    B. Peaceful and pleased

    C. Cold and shivering

CHAPTER 5   ADVENTURE IN THE NIGHT

"Come on out where I can see you," said Keith. *Pb-pb-b-b-b.* Ralph **shot** out into the moonlight, where he stopped, sitting on the motorcycle.

10. Which is the **correct** meaning of the word **shot** in this sentence?

    A. To discharge a firearm or bow

    B. To move quickly

    C. The range or distance traveled by a missile or bullet

    D. An injection by means of a needle

    E. A stroke in certain games as billiards or basketball

11. Why was Ralph frightened and hiding behind the ashtray near the elevator?

   A. Because outside an owl hooted, was silent, and hooted again.

   B. Because the morning sounds of birds in the pines grew louder.

   C. Because he had been seen by the dog.

Ralph had seen Matt many times, but his was the first time the old man had spoken to him. He was **astonished**.

12. What is the meaning of the word **astonished**?

   A. Unsurprised and aware

   B. Filled with overpowering surprise and wonder

   C. Tense and frightened

CHAPTER 6   A PEANUT BUTTER SANDWICH

13. What did Ralph promise Keith?

   A. Not to ride the motorcycle in the daytime

   B. Two peanut butter sandwiches

   C. To apologize to his mother

It must be terrible to go through life without fur and such a **nuisance**, having to wear clothes that had to be washed and drip-dried.

14. Which word means the **same** as **nuisance**?

   A. Advantage

   B. Pleasure

   C. Inconvenience

CHAPTER 7   THE VACUUM CLEANER

15. Why does Ralph break his promise to Keith?

   A. He and the motorcycle were in danger of being inhaled with the dust.

   B. He had to avoid the terrifying hole at the end of the tube.

   C. He wondered if the motor on the cycle was stronger than the pull of the vacuum machine.

It would be an important experiment. Motorcycle **versus** vacuum cleaner.

16. Which word means the **same** as **versus** in this sentence?

   A. Against

   B. Winner

   C. With

Ralph was filled with **remorse** at the loss of Keith's motorcycle.

17. What is the meaning of the word **remorse** in this sentence?

    A. Satisfaction and happiness

    B. Deep and painful regret for wrongdoing

    C. Tired and sleepy

CHAPTER 8   A FAMILY REUNION

18. Why had Ralph's aunts, uncles, and cousins come to visit?

    A. Because there would be a feast at the wedding.

    B. Because there was enough food for everyone.

    C. Because they were afraid of the dog.

19. Why was the motorcycle important to Keith?

    A. Because it was a present from his favorite uncle.

    B. Because he saved his allowance to buy it.

    C. Because he was old enough to be trusted with it.

Never in his whole life had Ralph felt so ashamed. He longed to crawl off into his hole and never face Keith again, but his **conscience** would not let him. There was nothing to do but **confess**.

20. What is the meaning of the word **conscience** in this context?

   A. The inner understanding that lets a person know when he is doing right or when he is doing wrong.
   B. Able to see, hear, feel; to awaken; to become aware of some object, fact, or feeling
   C. Ruthless and unreasonable

21. What does the word **confess** mean in this sentence?

   A. To deny or withhold information
   B. To acknowledge or reveal information
   C. To conceal important facts

CHAPTER 9   RALPH TAKES COMMAND

"I want to grow up and go down to the ground floor," said Ralph. "Everybody tells me to be **patient**," said Keith, "but I don't want to be **patient**."

22. Which is the correct meaning for **patient** in these sentences?

   A. A person who is under medical care or treatment

   B. Impatient, frustrated, or agitated

   C. Understanding and uncomplaining

23. What is the **problem** in this chapter?

   A. Hotel management will put out traps and poisons to capture mice.

   B. The owls could capture the mice.

   C. Ralph's brothers, sisters, and cousins gave awful and loud squeals.

24. What was Ralph's **solution** to their problem?

   A. The mice would leave the hotel.

   B. The mice would keep quiet for a few days.

   C. The mice would refuse food from the boy, Keith.

CHAPTER 10 AN ANXIOUS NIGHT

25. How does Ralph try to help Keith?

   A. He reported the news to his relatives.

   B. He climbed to the windowsill to look for owls.

   C. He decided to find an aspirin tablet in the hotel.

From his **perch** on the windowsill Ralph saw that the parking lot held more cars than usual.

26. What is the meaning of the word **perch** in this context?

   A. Any of several fresh-water fishes used as food.

   B. A place to sit, settle or rest in an elevated position

   C. A pole, branch, or bar used as a roost for birds

CHAPTER 11   THE SEARCH

His entire family stared at him in **disbelief**. Not an aspirin! Not after his own father had been poisoned by one of the dread tablets.

27. Which word means the **opposite** of **disbelief** in this sentence?

    A. Unbelievingness

    B. Confidence, trust and certainty

    C. Amazement and astonishment

28. How did the teacher get rid of Ralph without hurting him?

    A. She used a drinking glass and clapped it down over him.

    B. She picked him up by the tail and put him into the hallway.

    C. She put a postcard under the glass and carried it to the window and shook Ralph off into the vines outside.

    D. She left him under the glass for the housekeeper to see.

CHAPTER 12   AN ERRAND OF MERCY

This carried him as he had planned to the elevator. It was a **crucial** moment. Now he would find out if his plan was going to work.

29. Which word means the **same** as **crucial** in this sentence?

   A. Necessary

   B. Unnecessary

   C. Insignificant

   D. optional

"Hey, Keith! I've got it!" Ralph was filled with **triumph**. "I've brought you an aspirin!"

30. Which **two** words mean the **same** as **triumph** in this sentence?

   A. Sorrow

   B. Elation

   C. Victorious

   D. Unhappiness

CHAPTER 13   A   SUBJECT FOR A   COMPOSITION

31. Who returned the lost motorcycle?

   A. The housekeeper

   B. Matt, the bellboy

   C. The desk clerk

32. Why did Keith allow Ralph to ride the motorcycle again?

   A. Because Ralph proved he was responsible when he found an aspirin

   B. Because Ralph hid his crash helmet behind the curtain

   C. Because Ralph had a daydream about riding it again

"And when the teacher asks us to write a **composition** about our summer vacation, I can write about meeting a brave mouse named Ralph who rode a little motorcycle." Keith said.

33. Which is the correct meaning for the word **composition** in this context?

   A. The act of putting together or combining parts to make a whole

   B. The thing that is put together as a piece of music

   C. A short essay written as a school exercise or assignment

   D. Architecture

Quietly Ralph parked the motorcycle beside the bed and quietly he removed his crash helmet and hid it behind the curtain. He did not want to **disturb** the sleeping boy.

34. Which word means the **same** as **disturb** in this sentence?

    A. Enlighten

    B. Bother

    C. Assist

35. Which **clue** in the **context** helps to understand the word **disturb**?

    A. Removed

    B. Quietly

    C. Parked

RALPH S. MOUSE

by Beverly Cleary

Ralph, the motorcycle-riding mouse, is off on another adventure and acquires a new sports car to replace his broken motorcycle.

CHAPTER 1   A DARK AND SNOWY NIGHT

Above Ralph the clock began to grind and groan and **strike**, *bong . . . bong.*

1. Which is the **correct** meaning for **strike** in the **context** of this sentence?

    A. In baseball, a pitch that the batter misses

    B. To attack or assault, as in the military, or with a fist or weapon

    C. To sound by percussion; to indicate time by the sound of a bell

    D. Stopping work or withdrawal of services

    E. To start burning or to ignite with a match

2. Why did Ralph grasp his tail?

    A. To avoid the clutching paws of his relatives

    B. So that it would not become tangled in the spokes

    C. To avoid the desk clerk stepping on it

"Try and make us." The outdoor mice were **defiant**.

3. What is the meaning of the word **defiant**?

    A. Boldly resistant and challenging

    B. Obedient

    C. Ashamed

CHAPTER 2   RALPH'S DECISION

4. Why did Ralph **feel** brave and noble?

   A. Because leaving the hotel would protect the safety of his little relatives

   B. Because he had no time to say good-by to Matt

   C. Because inside the pocket was cozy

CHAPTER 3   IRWIN J. SNEED ELEMENTARY SCHOOL

Ralph wondered how he could **endure** a whole day of waiting for night to come so he could race down that long hall.

5. Which word means the **same** as **endure** in this sentence?

   A. To tolerate and stick it out

   B. To surrender

   C. To disapprove

6. Why did Ralph **feel** both guilty and **doomed**?

   A. Miss K thought he was a beautiful mouse.

   B. He had broken his promise to stay out of sight.

   C. He didn't know people gnawed things too.

7. Which word means the **opposite** of **doomed** as used in this sentence?

   A. Overwhelmed

   B. Ill-fated

   C. Hopeful

   D. unfortunate

"You have to run the maze," said Ryan. Ralph became **stubborn**, "No, I don't," he **contradicted**, "and you can't make me."

8. What is the meaning of the word **contradict** in this sentence?

   A. Deny and oppose

   B. Support

   C. Ignored

9. Which words mean the **same** as <u>**stubborn**</u> in this sentence?

   A. Determined and unshakeable

   B. Submissive and surrendering

   C. Yielding and willing

Ralph wanted his motorcycle, but Ryan said, "We'll see about that, after you run the race on Friday." With that **ultimatum** stated, he hurried to catch the bus.

10. What does the word **ultimatum** mean in this sentence?

    A. A terrible feeling

    B. A final statement or proposal of conditions

    C. Ultimate concerns of injury

CHAPTER 4   LIFE AT SCHOOL

11. What did Ralph do just **before** he chewed into a bag of sugar while exploring?

    A. He ran up the leg of Ryan's jeans and onto his shirt.

    B. He discovered a nutritious meal of split peas, rice, and lentils in Room 4.

    C. He found an open jar of library paste.

    D. He discovered something interesting on a bottom shelf behind a big desk.

CHAPTER 5   THE GREAT MOUSE EXHIBIT

12. Ralph curled up in a tight ball to stop his trembling. **Why** is he trembling?

    A. He was horrified that a brown mouse died in Gloria's poem.

    B. He was afraid that he would harm the motorcycle.

    C. He was cold and shivering.

"Now our guest of honor will **demonstrate** how quickly he can learn," said Miss K.

13. Which word means the **same** as the word **demonstrate** in this sentence?

    A. Explain and argue

    B. Display and show

    C. Hide and seek

CHAPTER   6   THE MAZE

14. What happened to Ralph's motorcycle in this chapter?

    A. It wrecked when he crashed into a wall.

    B. It was destroyed when Ryan and Brad had a fight.

    C. Brad smashed it because Ralph raced across the top of the maze.

15. Why did the children **not** return to school?

   A. Because they were disappointed that Ralph could not run the maze

   B. Because it was a holiday

   C. Because there was no school on Saturday and Sunday

Ralph had never been so alone in his life. All weekend he roamed the **desolate** halls and classrooms.

16. Which word means the **same** as **desolate** in this sentence?

   A. Delighted

   B. Abandoned

   C. Populated

   D. befriended

CHAPTER 7   THE   CUCARACHA   VOICE

17. Why were the students **upset** about the article in the newspaper?

   A. The snow began to melt by Monday morning.

   B. The reported got it all wrong. It made the school sound terrible.

   C. Ralph was expected to run the maze again.

CHAPTER 8   RALPH   SPEAKS

18. What sort of person understands Ralph?

    A. A gifted and talented student

    B. One who is lonesome and interested in cars

    C. All students in elementary school

Ralph found himself once again in the fishbowl, furious with Ryan for not managing to save him from this **indignity**.

19. How does Ralph **feel** about being in the fishbowl?

    A. Humiliated and insulted

    B. Complimented and honored

    C. Cheerful and delighted

CHAPTER 9   THE SURPRISE

20. What was the **surprise** in this chapter?

    A. Brad gave Ralph a car to replace the broken motorcycle

    B. The students gave Miss K a cake for her birthday

    C. Matt, the bellboy, had not lost his job

The editors of the newspaper **regret** any embarrassment caused Room 5 by the misleading article about their activities.

21. What does the word **regret** mean in this sentence?

    A. Offer apologies

    B. Express happiness

    C. Shares confusion

The car was low enough, if **maneuvered** by a skillful driver, to slip through the bottom of the clock.

22. Which **two** words mean the same as **maneuvered** in this sentence?

    A. Navigated

    B. Destroyed

    C. Neglected

    D. Manipulated

EPILOGUE

23. What was the **unexpected** outcome or **ending** of this novel?

    A. The boys became brothers after Brad's dad and Ryan's mom were married.

    B. Ralph decided to return to school and remain their forever.

    C. Ralph is the only mouse who sits in the driver's seat of the Laser XL7.

HATCHET

by   Gary Paulsen

After a plane crash, thirteen-year-old Brian spends 54 days in the wilderness, learning to survive initially with only the aid of a hatchet given to him by his mother, and learning also to survive his parent's divorce.

1

The **vibration** of the plane came through the wheel and the pedals.

1. Which word means the **same** as **vibration** in this sentence?

    A. Stillness

    B. Shaking

    C. Gliding

2. Why is Brian on the plane? Where is he going?

    A. To visit his dad for the summer

    B. To learn how to fly as a copilot in the cockpit

    C. To learn how to make emergency landings correctly

2

3. What did Brian need to do **before** he could use the radio?

    A. Adjust the wheel to avoid crashing

    B. Get the headset from the pilot

    C. Reach the pilot's belt to release the switch

4. How is Brian **feeling** after half an hour without help?

    A. Adventurous and awesome

    B. Bored and brave

    C. Frustrated and frightened

3

5. Where did the plane land?

    A. In the L-shaped lake

    B. In a small pond

    C. In a wide space leading to the lake

4

6. What **secret** memory did Brian have?

    A. Seeing his mother sitting in a car with another man

    B. Seeing his dad sitting in a car with another woman

    C. Skipping school with his friend Terry

7. Why didn't Brian have very much energy?

   A. Because his body was in some kind of shock from the crash

   B. Because he was drained from swatting flies and mosquitos

   C. Because he had to swim a couple of miles to get out of the water

8. What did Brian need to do **first** to help himself?

   A. Find or make a weapon for protection

   B. Run away from the mosquitos and flies

   C. Have some kind of shelter and have something to eat

"You are your most valuable **asset**. You are the best thing you have."

9. What is the meaning of the word **asset** in this sentence?

   A. Advantage or benefit

   B. Disadvantage

   C. Problem

6

He wanted to stay near the lake. He didn't want to **diminish** any chance he might have of being found.

10. Which word means the **same** as **diminish** as used in this sentence?

    A. Raise and praise

    B. Decrease or lessen

    C. Develop and enlarge

11. What did Brian do to **solve** his problems in this chapter? (2 answers)

    A. He started a fire with driftwood and dead dry branches.

    B. He found berries to satisfy his hunger and thirst.

    C. He had a shelter almost fifteen feet long and ten feet deep.

    D. He caught fish and fried them to eat.

7

12. Why was Brian vomiting and have terrible diarrhea?

    A. The lake water was not purified.

    B. He had eaten to many berries and pits.

    C. The mosquito bites had poisoned his blood.

13. Why did Brian decide to go back to the raspberry patch?

    A. Because he was no longer afraid of the bear

    B. Because he did not want to eat the tart gut berries again

    C. Because he did not want the birds and squirrels to eat all of them

8

14. What did Brian learn is the **most important** rule of survival?

    A. It is dangerous to be alone at night without any fire.

    B. Self-pity accomplishes nothing. Feeling sorry for yourself doesn't work.

    C. A light sleep or doze is better than a deep sleep.

15. What important event occurred at the **end** of this chapter?

    A. Brian's father and friend Terry visited him in his dreams.

    B. It is better to jerk porcupine quills and remove them quickly from his leg.

    C. He used sparks from the stone in the cave and his hatchet to make a fire.

9

There had to be something for the sparks to **ignite**, some kind of kindling.

16. What is the meaning of the word **ignite** in this sentence?

   A. Extinguish

   B. Inflame or burn

   C. quench

17. How was the fire beneficial to Brian?

   A. It was like a pet to feed.

   B. It was like a friend and a guard.

   C. It was scarry and threatening.

10

Brian made certain the fire was **banked** with new wood, then left the shelter.

18. Which is the **correct** meaning of **banked** as used in this sentence?

   A. The land along the edge of a river or stream

   B. To put or keep money in a bank

   C. Put in a pile or mound

19. What is Brian's wonderful discovery about fire?

    A. Mosquitos and bugs were never near the smoke and fire.

    B. It made the shelter feel like home.

    C. It crackled with colorful flames.

20. What did Brian do immediately **after** he ate six eggs?

    A. He stored the rest of the eggs in the shelter.

    B. He decided to only eat one egg a day.

    C. He ripped the shells open and licked the insides clean.

    D. He wondered if he could eat the shells.

The hunger, always there, had been somewhat controlled and **dormant** when there was nothing to eat but with the eggs came the scream to eat.

21. What is the meaning of **dormant** as used in this sentence?

    A. Closed-down, inactive

    B. Alert and active

    C. Conscious

11

22. Why was it necessary for Brian to keep busy?

    A. So, he would not get depressed thinking about how they hadn't found him.

    B. Because it took all of his will to keep from eating all of the eggs.

    C. Because he wanted his camp area always clean and tidy.

23. What **changes** about himself had Brian noticed? (2 answers)

    A. He had grown a foot taller since the plane crashed.

    B. His senses of sight and sound were stronger and better than ever.

    C. He had lost some weight around the middle and stomach area.

    D. He like the way the light moved with the ripples of the water.

12

24. What is Brian's **goal** in this chapter?

    A. Be ready to light a fire if he heard a plane engine.

    B. To make a bow and arrow to catch fish.

    C. To find another location for his shelter.

25. How does Brian **feel** at the **end** of this chapter? (2 answers)

   A. Excited to add grass and chips to the flames so the bonfire was as high as his head.

   B. Disappointed that the search plane was gone.

   C. Hopeless, he didn't he would see his family again.

   D. Brave to be living alone in the wilderness.

13

26. What **life changing decision** did Brian make?

   A. He would not die; he would not let death in his heart again.

   B. He would smile even though he had made a lot of mistakes.

   C. He spent a whole night to shape the bow and two days making arrows.

   D. He used a shoelace for a bowstring.

27. What is Brian's new **hope** at the **end** of this chapter?

   A. Hope that he would be eventually rescued.

   B. Hope in the fact he could learn and survive to take care of himself.

   C. Hope to have another feast of twenty delicious fish to eat.

28. Forty-seven days had passed since the crash. How many **weeks** is this?

    A. About six weeks

    B. About seven weeks

    C. About eight weeks

14

Small mistakes could turn into disasters.

In the city if he made a mistake usually there was a way to **rectify** it, make it right.

29. What is the meaning of the word **rectify** as used in this sentence?

    A. Destroy

    B. Correct

    C. Corrupt

30. What did Brian do **after** the skunk sprayed him?

    A. He screamed and quickly ran out of the shelter.

    B. He scrambled into the water to wash his eyes.

    C. He laughed thinking about cute cartoons with skunks.

31. Why did Brian need a ladder?

    A. To get away from a bear

    B. To reach a ledge above the shelter

    C. To sit on top of the shelter to enjoy the view

15

32. How did Brian **solve** the problem of camouflage?

    A. He hid behind a tree and waited for the fool-birds to walk by.

    B. He had trained his eyes to see the shape and outline of these birds.

    C. He used the spear and not the bow and arrow to hunt them.

33. What **life lesson** did Brian learn in this chapter?

    A. Patience and thinking

    B. Bruised but not broken

    C. Avoid self-pity

16

34. What **caused** the pain in Brian's ribs in this chapter?

    A. He was attacked by a bear.

    B. He was attacked by a group of squirrels.

    C. He was attacked by a moose.

    D. He was attacked by mosquitos and flies again.

17

35. Which is the **best outcome** of all after the inspection of the tornado damage?

    A. He had not been killed or seriously injured.

    B. He finally had enough wood to keep the fire going.

    C. Most of the wood from his wall was nearby.

36. **After** he made a raft, what **problem** did he have at the **end** of this chapter?

   A. He could not find the survival bag.

   B. He could not get inside of the plane.

   C. He could not see inside because the water was murky.

18

37. What did Brian discover **after** he slammed his fist against the plane?

   A. The aluminum covering moved and bent easily.

   B. Nothing out here in this place is easy.

   C. He might be able to force his way inside.

38. How did Brian **feel** at the **end** of this chapter?

   A. Triumphantly and victorious

   B. Defeated and rejected

   C. Dumbfounded and confused

Unbelievable riches. He could not believe the **contents** of the survival pack.

39. Which is the **correct** meaning of **contents** as used in this context?

   A. Subjects or topics covered in a book

   B. A significance or profound meaning

   C. All that a thing contains, hold, or include

   D. Happy enough not to complain, satisfaction

At that **precise** instant, with his mind full of home and smell from the food filing him, the plane appeared.

40. Which is the meaning of **precise** as used in this sentence?

   A. Unsuitable

   B. Questionable

   C. Exact

41. What **caused** Brian to be rescued?

   A. A plane appeared after seeing smoke from Brian's feast

   B. The pilot received a signal from the emergency transmitter.

   C. Everyone had been looking for Brian for months.

THE REAL THIEF

By   William Steig

When Gawain the goose is deserted by his friends after being unjustly convicted of stealing from his beloved king, the real thief is tortured by his conscience.

PAGES 9-29

Whenever the King removed anything from the treasury, he informed Gawain of the changes. Gawain always enjoyed these short **conferences**.

1. What is the **correct** meaning of the word **conferences** in this sentence?

    A. An association of athletic teams, a league

    B. a group of churches whose representative regularly meet in an assembly

    C. A meeting for consultation or discussion

2. Why is Gawain a suspect for taking the missing rubies and jewels?

    A. Because only Gawain and the king have keys to the Royal Treasury

    B. Because Gawain was careless in his duties

    C. Because the King makes no mistakes

    D. Because the other two guards had witnesses of their whereabouts

I cannot vouch for your highness, only for myself. It wasn't I.

Gawain could hear the crowd gasp. He knew that his **audacity** had shocked them.

3. What is the meaning of **audacity** as used in this sentence?

    A. Caring and meekness

    B. Boldness, daring confidence

    C. Adventurous

"You are a disgrace to this kingdom!" said Basil with disgust.

"Why are they all looking at me with such **aversion**?" Gawain asked himself.

4. Which word means the **same** as **aversion** as used in this sentence?

    A. Dissatisfaction

    B. Affection

    C. Approval

5. What did Gawain do at the **end** of this section of the story?

    A. He admitted to his guilt and pleaded for mercy.

    B. He accused beaver John of being a liar and a thief.

    C. He escaped imprisonment by flying out of a window.

PAGES 31-49

6. Why did Derek, a mouse, steal more gems?

    A. Because greed and envy was very important to him
    B. Because it made him feel like a mouse of importance
    C. Because he has dreams of being the king one day

7. Why did Derek decide to steal silver items from the treasury?

    A. Because the silver was more artfully and creative.
    B. Because he needed something other than warm colors in his house.
    C. Because he desired a better center of attention.

He rolled the diamond along the stone floor, and when he reached the **crevice**, it dropped through. He rolled it into his house.

8. Which word means the **same** as **crevice**?

    A. Hole
    B. Closing
    C. Corner

9. How did everyone **feel** *after* the treasure was returned?

   A. Joyful and happy

   B. Miserable

   C. Powerful

Derek decided he would confess. He would go straight to the King, make **restitution**, and take his punishment.

10. What is the meaning of **restitution**?

    A. To fix or correct; to make amends

    B. It is a penalty for perjury

    C. Refusing to admit guilt

Vindicating Gawain was the first good work Derek had done since he'd become a thief. It eased his misery, but only briefly.

11. What does it mean to vindicate someone?

    A. To incriminate

    B. Prove one's innocence

    C. To deny

12. The *cloud of gloom* that hung over the whole kingdom hung the thickest over Derek. Why?

    A. Because he was guilty of the crime that falsely accused Gawain
    B. Because Gawain's name had been cleared of any wrongdoing
    C. Because carting the loot from his home to the treasury was hard labor.

PAGES   51-66

Gawain tied rushes (stems) to his webbed feed and walked about **obliterating** the imprint he had made in the damp soil.

13. What does **obliterate** mean in this sentence?

    A. To ignore
    B. To exterminate
    C. To erase, mark out, cover

Gawain took up the life of a fugitive and a **recluse**, with only himself for company.

14. What makes Gawain a **recluse**?

    A. He withdraws from the world to live alone.
    B. Very sociable
    C. He has many friends.

"I think you have been punished for what you did." Gawain said to Derek.

"You were the one wrongfully blamed," said Derek.

"But you had it on your **conscience** that you caused the suffering of so many," said Gawain.

15. What does it mean to have a **conscience**?

    A. To have an inner sense of right and wrong
    B. To be unashamed
    C. To never know the answer

16. What happened **after** Gawain and Derek returned to the kingdom?

    A. Gawain was given his old job back.
    B. Derek became the new king.
    C. There was peace and harmony once again.

17. Why did Derek secretly cement the chink in the floor of the treasury?

    A. So, he wouldn't be tempted to steal again.
    B. Because it made him feel better.
    C. Because it was necessary to survive.

ABOUT THE AUTHOR

Credentials: Principal (Administrator) Certification   EC–12

Master of Education: Curriculum & Instruction

Bachelor of Science in Elementary Education   1 – 8

English as a Second Language Certification

Experience: Classroom Teacher   29 years

ESL Pull-Out Teacher   2 years

Instructional Coach   2 years

Encourage students to go to the public library and their school library for novels.

Parents and grandparents can purchase books online and in stores where books are sold.

- ✓ Research shows that children who read at least 20 minutes a day are exposed to about 2 million words per year.

Books by Doris McKelvey

Mckelvey.doris@yahoo.com

Devotionals:
- Text Messages from God
- The Decision: Life or Death
- Secret Things
- A Relationship with Jesus
- Ladies of Strength
- Forgiving Grudges: No More Bitterness

Christian Fiction: Distractions   Good-Night Liz

Education: Independent Reading Workbook Grades 3-8

Made in the USA
Middletown, DE
30 March 2024